Rolf F. Rehe   **Typography: how to make it most legible**

Typography: how to make it most legible

Rolf F. Rehe

Design Research Publications

Indianapolis

Design Research Publications
P.O.B. 27
Carmel, Indiana 46032

Index

Index (Cont.)

Acknowledgments

This book was originally produced in partial fulfillment of the requirements for the degree, Master of Arts, in the Department of Journalism, Indiana University. I wish to express my sincere gratitude to those who have helped me with the project.

The chairman of my thesis committee, Professor Wil Counts (Journalism), and committee members Professor Jack Backer (Journalism), Professor Tom Coleman (Graphic Design), and Professor Poynter McEvoy (Journalism), provided most valuable assistance, patiently discussed problems related to the project with me, and gave me the benefit of their rich experiences.

Professor Joseph Lucca (Graphic Design) helped me with the original outline of the project and encouraged me to proceed. Charles Abel, President of Rogers Typesetting, Indianapolis, Indiana, aided me with the production aspects of the project. Ann Miller helped with the research and the typing of the copy. G. Harvey Petty, typographer, read the entire manuscript and made many helpful suggestions. Friedemann K. Bartsch assisted me with the editing of the material and with the proofreading chores.

I am most grateful for the assistance given to me by these individuals and hope the completed project justifies their contributions.

R.F.R.

1 The need for a functional typography

A print shop during the Middle Ages.

Most all of the scribes of medieval Europe were monks. For them, producing books was a work of art, an attempt to please God with beautiful lettering. Concern about communicating was generally a secondary issue. When the honorable burgher of Mainz, Johannes Gutenberg, invented movable type and thus industrialized book production, he copied, in his first type designs, the hand lettering of the scribes. The justified line, with its miraculously even word spacing, was achieved with the aid of a large number of ligature letters and abbreviations, marking the shortened words with a horizontal bar above the letters.

> in exterminiū: ꝫ ꝗ a nobis eſt iter exter-
> miniṷ: illi autē ſunt in pace. Er ſi corā
> hoibus rozmēta paſſi ſunt: ſpes illoꝛ

Type from the 42-line Gutenberg Bible.

In general, the basic approach to typography has not undergone major changes since the days of Gutenberg. This stylistic stagnation resulted from the unchanging technical methods of producing type and typography. The horizontal linearity of typesetting and the

9

The Hoe Type Revolving Machine.

methods of putting type together in a form (later to be speeded up by the invention of typesetting machines) have, in principle, remained since the craftsman of Mainz invented movable type. There were the printing techniques, simple platen presses, later supplemented by the cylinder presses. At times even the new presses forced additional restrictions on typography. The Hoe Type Revolving Machine, for instance, required newspapers to have vertical rules between the columns to hold the type locked onto the cylinder. Consequently, newspaper typography was restricted to setting and arranging type in single columns with single column headlines.

A typical newspaper of 1846, with one-column makeup, and vertical column rules keeping the form locked to the press.

Typesetting itself was a tedious and time consuming task. In large composing rooms, small armies of compositors set all type for publications by hand, distributing the forms by hand after printing. There were the limitations of established type forms, page widths, galleys, and press beds. New type creations over the centuries brought with them minor stylistic changes of typographic arrangement. But it was usually the full, justified line, arranged in

10

standard patterns, printed in standard type sizes, that dominated typographic forms.

The technological-typographical revolution

Then came the technological-typographical revolution. Ottmar Mergenthaler invented the Linotype machine, capable of producing the work of many compositors in short time. In Bavaria, the unemployed actor Alois Senefelder accidentally discovered the principle of lithographic printing, later to become sophisticated into the high-speed offset technique. Finally, the years after World War II brought the development of speedy, flexible photocomposition methods. Photo-typesetting provided the technical possibilities for a design revolution. With the cold type pasteup technique, restrictions imposed traditionally by standard widths of spacing material, galley sizes, chase forms, and most other restrictions inherent in metal typesetting, have disappeared.

Originally, the production of printed matter was of a small scale. Ratio of printing produced in comparison to the size of the population was low. People had much time and read leisurely. Only a small part of the citizenry knew how to read.

But gradually, especially in the 20th century, a new situation has evolved. The level of education has risen dramatically. Much more information is being transmitted. Reading speed and comprehension have become important factors in the communication process. Not all the print communication produced, in fact, only a small part of it, can be absorbed by the average reader for simple reasons of time. Printed messages now compete for the reader's attention and interest. Speedy transmission of printed communication has become an important determinant of the message's acceptance by the reader. Typography emerged as a functional aspect of print communication.

Scientific investigation of typography appears

At about the turn of this century, an important factor contributing to the development of a new, functional typography appeared: the scientific investigation of typographic legibility. Primarily psychologists studied the ways by which printed type is perceived, and what arrangements and forms of type provide maximum legibility.

The first serious investigation of legibility is thought to have begun with Professor Emile Javal of the University of Paris in 1878. Javal tried to establish the legibility of individual letters of the alphabet by distance tests and visibility trials. In the years following, sporadic research was conducted, but concentrated research into legibility on a broader scale evolved in the years around 1920.

Today, the range of investigators includes journalists, educators, computer-scientists, governmental agencies, and the graphic arts industry in general.

The areas investigated concern mainly the problem of increasing reading speed and comprehension, that is, finding the typographic arrangement best facilitating these factors, and finding such typographic variables which please the eye and achieve reader attention and response.

The importance of effective typography

In our communication-conscious time, these factors are of vital importance in conveying information via the typographic medium. For one, with an ever increasing amount of print information confronting contemporary man, a selective process is necessary by the reader since it is impossible to consume all print information made available. In addition to relying on contextual clues, the reader depends on the typographical makeup when selecting print information for actual reading. Printing that, in a pleasing way, attracts the reader's eye will have a better chance of being read than a piece of print communication presented in a dull, unattractive typography.

Secondly, to permit the reader to absorb as much print information as possible, the economy of typographic communication, that is, reading speed, needs to be improved. Some of the studies presented here will show that substantial gains in reading speed can be achieved with a typography applying research findings from legibility studies.

The typographer as mass communicator

Originally, the typographer was typecaster, typesetter, and printer all in one person. As printing and typesetting became specialized, a division of labor emerged. Perhaps the evolution of the typographer as a specialist was fostered by the Bauhaus group of designers during the first 3 decades of the 20th century. They challenged traditional forms of typography with the motto, ''Form follows function.'' Actual typographic design increasingly became the task of specialists who usually had a technical as well as a design background and were therefore familiar with all aspects of typographic production.

However, even today only a few typographic designers have taken advantage of available research findings in legibility. A frequent complaint by researchers is that their findings have not been widely applied in the design of typographic communications. Part of the problem stems from the fact that most research results have been

KASIMIR MALEWITSCH
**DIE
GEGENSTANDSLOSE
WELT**

BAUHAUSBÜCHER 11

A typical book cover in the functional Bauhaus style.

published in scientific journals, usually in a vernacular not easily understood by the typographer.

The typographer in a mass media age, it seems, needs to be well schooled not only in the aesthetical aspects of design, but also in the technical aspects and possibilities of modern typesetting and printing methods. He needs, additionally, to be acquainted with the psychology of typography, the techniques and results of legibility research, and with his own role in the communications process.

The role of the typographer

In a mass media system, the typographer is usually a member of the encoding team. He stands between the original source of the message and the channel (here: the printed page), which will carry the message to an audience. He has considerable control over the coding process by selecting type faces, type sizes, and by determining the typographic arrangement of the message. He should be concerned with the perception of his message, the attention it can elicit, the mood it creates, its legibility and degree of comprehension, with maintaining the reader's attention after it has been attained initially, and with a high degree of recall by the reader. Partly his task is one of metacommunication, communicating messages about the message, transmitted often simultaneously. He is, in short, not any longer a designer of aesthetic printing, or simply an artist or craftsman. The typographer of today is a mass communicator, playing an important role in the mass media system.

In a simplified mass media model, typography contributes in the encoding stage, influences channel transmission, and helps

determine perception, selection, and comprehension of the
message:

SENDER	CHANNEL	RECEIVER
Encoding: graphic and typographic design based on legibility research and related psychological factors	Interferences of the transmission of the message may be caused by "noise" or "blur" (poor design, smeared printing, etc.)	Decoding: this process may be improved by design based on human trends in perception, factors of legibility, comprehension, appeal, and many more.

The importance of typography within the context of print media design finds increased recognition. Typographic message packaging has become an important determinant of whether a print communication is selected and read — and read completely.

It is the purpose of this booklet to provide the typographic media man, and anyone else interested in typographic message packaging, with a set of recommendations for a more functional, more communicative typography.

When carefully applied, these recommendations should improve both attention impact and reading speed as well as comprehension of typographic messages by the reader.

2 Research methods and approach

Research into legibility of print may be one of the oldest forms of research in the communications field. The earliest legibility research may have been a count of words and ideas conducted by the Talmudists around 900 A.D., using frequency of word occurrence as a means of distinguishing usual from unusual meaning of words, Neman (87) reports.

Systematic research into legibility of print began in the late 19th century with Javal's pioneer study, attempting to determine the relative legibility of individual letters of the alphabet. Roethlein (116) conducted a similar, extensive study into the legibility of individual letters. During these pioneer stages of legibility research, emphasis was placed on investigation of individual letters and their visibility. Size and width of letters, height of type, and relative alphabet length were subjects of elaborate studies.

Around 1920, research into legibility flourished. A wide variety of factors relative to legibility was investigated by psychologists, ophthalmologists, educators, and journalists. A controversy about the value of certain systems of methodology was carried out in many journal articles. At one time, illumination (optimal light conditions) was of major interest to the researchers, the intensity of the light usually measured by the number of wax candles used. Today, with good light conditions a standard, research into illumination has become extinct.

The most recent trend in legibility research seems to emphasize investigations which produce results directly applicable to typographic design.

With the founding of the **International Committee on Legibility Research** and the appearance of publications related to typographic legibility, attempts have been made to coordinate and communicate legibility research.

How the eye perceives the printed word

To understand the bulk of legibility research conducted, it may be helpful to illustrate how the printed word is perceived by the human eye.

This is an example of how eye (saccadic) movements may progress during reading. Circles indicate the focusing points for each stop (fixation), while the squares show the approximate area covered by the eye during a fixation. Broken lines indicate saccadic jumps, and solid lines are (re-reading) regressions.

An illustration of how reading matter may be perceived by the human eye, based on a graph by Wendt (177).

When reading, the eye sweeps along the line of print in so-called saccadic jumps. In regular intervals, it pauses quickly (for about ¼ of a second), and it is during that short pause or fixation that actual perception of words takes place. After the short pause, the eye proceeds with another saccadic movement, then pauses again to perceive and comprehend the words. Occasionally the eye might move back on the line to re-read what might not have been comprehended adequately the first time. Return moves are termed "regressions."

Tinker (135) found that the proportion of time taken by eye movements varies with comprehension demands of the reading situation. Pause or perception time usually involved 92 to 94% of reading time.

The methods of measuring legibility

To measure legibility, 8 basic methods of measurement have been established. In addition to these methods, a number of unique measuring devices exist.

The following outline of the 8 standard methods of measuring legibility will be general and brief. It seems more advantageous for the typographic designer to present research results, rather than to elaborate on experimental procedures. However, so that experimental details may be studied, reference will be made to the individual studies by numbers in parentheses ( ). Detailed referential information may then be found in the bibliography at the end of this booklet.

Speed of perception is measured by a short-exposure technique. Printed matter is briefly (i.e., $1/10$ of a second) exposed to a subject by the tachistoscope, a special instrument designed for this purpose. This method has been applied primarily in experiments investigating the legibility of individual letters and symbols, and in the field of word-perception research.

Perceptibility at a distance is a method which measures the distance from which letters and symbols may be perceived. This method, too, has found application primarily in investigations into the legibility of individual letters and symbols, and has been used to test the legibility of posters, road signs, etc.

Perceptibility at peripheral vision and the vocal variator investigate the horizontal distance from which print can be perceived, and the distance by which typographic matter can be thrown out of focus and still be recognized. The method has found limited application in the measurement of individual letters and symbols.

The visibility method employs a visibility meter, which is basically a set of filters through which the subject views printed material. The density of the filter provides the measurement of perception. The method has found application primarily for studies of individual letters and symbols.

With the **reflex-blink technique,** the reader's frequency of blinking is counted, either manually or photographic-electronically. It is assumed that poor legibility of type will result in increased blinking. The validity and reliability of this method has been questioned frequently.

The rate-of-work technique measures reading speed, such as amount of reading within a given time limit, or time of reading for a given amount of text. Comprehension checks after the reading measure accuracy of reading in this method. Miles A. Tinker sees it as the best method of measurement available, and it is perhaps the most frequently employed method of measuring legibility.

The measurement of eye movements provides good clues to the understanding of legibility factors in typography. The method provides information such as why a certain typographic arrangement is perceived positively or negatively by showing the fixation pauses, their duration, and the regressions. Eye movements are recorded photographically or electronically. This measuring method, too, is considered an excellent one. Measuring eye movements, however, can be a very tedious task.

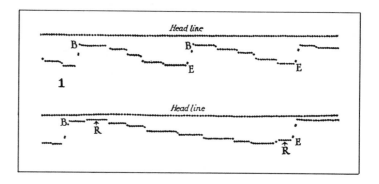

Recording of eye movements: Tinker (135) shows a good reader (above), and a poor reader (below).

Fatigue in reading has been investigated extensively, but research has not provided significant clues to legibility. Anderson/Meredith (2) have shown that readers can sustain several hours uninterrupted reading without significant signs of fatigue.

The 8 methods of measurement can provide relatively reliable data on the legibility of print. It needs to be pointed out, however, that all methods are only relatively accurate, since measurement of perception includes a variety of uncontrolled factors.

A generally new area of typographic research, the investigation of congeniality, or atmosphere-value of printing type, combines different methods of investigation. Detailed reference to these methods will be made in a following chapter.

The majority of studies consists of univariate analysis, that is, only one typographic variable was investigated at a time. But obviously, in typography, a variety of variables interact. As a rule, isolated research findings may be applied with good results, but it is suggested to combine research findings where possible. For instance, type size, line width, and leading should always be considered together since these variables greatly inter-relate.

Selection of studies

How were the studies in legibility selected for this project? First of all, out of the great bulk of research dealing either directly or in a marginal way with legibility, only such experiments were selected which, in the opinion of the author, were directly applicable to typographic design. Most of the studies employed one of the 8 methods of measuring legibility mentioned earlier. Application of one of the 8 methods does not automatically guarantee a sound design of an experiment. But it is felt that at least some control, relative as it may be, is being obtained. The small number of experiments which employ methods of measurement other than the 8 listed before were judged by their individual merits.

Research findings were then grouped into categories of typographic variables which are loosely based on a list made up by Bror Zachrisson (183), the Swedish legibility expert. They are: (1) type: individual letters, boldness, caps versus lower case, Roman versus italics, etc.; (2) length of line; (3) amount of leading; (4) color and contrast; (5) typographic arrangement; (6) size of typographical elements.

The recommendations

Recommendations for application of research findings are then made in the following form:

(1) **Recommendations based on research results** and supported by at least 2 research findings which have investigated the same typographic variables and produced similar results. When at least 2 research results support an optimal typographic variable, a reasonable case may be made for application of that variable. In the text, recommendations are designated by ■.

(2) **Proposals which are based on only one research finding.** While the value of a single investigation is somewhat relative, it is felt that by providing these proposals, the decision for application depends on the specific typographic situation. In this booklet, such proposals are indicated by ●.

(3) **Proposals based on recommendations made by researchers,** often on the basis of their own research. These proposals may not necessarily be supported by experimental evidence, but, in the judgment of this investigator, may provide practical and reasonable suggestions for an effective typography. They are designated by ★ in this text.

Limitations of the research findings have been pointed out earlier. All findings need to be applied carefully, especially if they are supported by fewer than 2 contributing studies. The results are best to be seen as aiding factors in typographic design, and not as automatic guarantors of maximum legibility. But applied with care, research results in form of recommendations and proposals may aid the typographic designer in creating a more effective mode of typographic communication.

3   Research findings and recommendations

To understand the many factors contributing to legibility, it might be helpful to look at some studies which have investigated the perception of individual letters by the eye. Research of individual letters, it may be recalled, was emphasized during the pioneer stages of legibility research.

While research of isolated letters does not take into account the situation arising when letters are combined to form words, this research adds greatly to our understanding of how the printed word is perceived. That understanding may serve as a valuable aid in typographic design.

Legibility of individual letters

The width of individual letters contributes to legibility. Condensed type designs are somewhat more difficult to read than moderately extended type design. When selected letters of "normal width" alphabet were slightly extended, their legibility generally increased, Berger (16) showed.

To some extent, the space around individual letters influences legibility. Additionally, the white space within letters (such as in o, e, c, etc.) influences their recognition, Roethlein (116) found. These

(1) dmpqw

(2) ceinl

Letters of high (1) and low (2) legibility.

light fight tight

light fight tight

light fight tight

An illustration of the perceivable similarity of letters in words of analogous outline shape.

letters, due to their similar shape, are often misread, and the white space within and around them helps to differentiate them.

Fine strokes of individual letters, a common feature in both Modern and Old Style Roman, tend to reduce legibility of individual letters by also reducing their differentiation value. Fine strokes have low visibility, and letters with fine strokes may be confused easily with other letters of similar shape, leading to reading errors, Tinker (149) discovered. The words "light" and "fight" provide an example of possible errors based on the wrong perception of individual key letters. Studies by Ovink (89), Sanford (118), and others showed that letters of poor legibility have a marked tendency to be misread and confused.

The optimal stroke width for individual letters should be about 18% of the total width or height of the letter, Uhlaner (171) reports.

Design of individual letters constitutes another important legibility factor. Two of the letters most frequently used in English, e and a, rank among the last in legibility of the letters of the alphabet, Sanford (118) found. The right half of individual letters, incidentally, is most significant for letter recognition.

Letters which have the right half obliterated.

Letters which have the left half obliterated. The right half of letters provides better cues for letter recognition.

Similarly, the upper halves of letters provide better cues for recognition, Paterson/Tinker (93), and Kolers (71) have shown.

The upper and lower halves of capital letters.

A redesign of many of the letters of the alphabet, resulting in better differentiation, has been recommended by several legibility researchers. On the basis of research into individual letter recognition, a prototype of a more legible alphabet has been suggested by Abelman (71). Emphasizing the right half of the letters for better recognition, the design may be seen more as an illustration of the problem rather than as a refined alternative.

A prototype design by Abelman, emphasizing the right half of letters.

In general, then, letters with specific differentiation are more easily recognized than letters without such differentiation. This finding applies to both serif and sans-serif type faces. News Gothic, for instance, with its somewhat differentiated sans-serif letters has been found to be more legible than other, more geometrically designed sans-serif type faces without specific letter differentiation, Poulton (110) found. A type face emphasizing individual letter differentiation for a sans-serif has been designed by Meyer (120).

Linear-Grotesk by H. E. Meyer, purportedly designed to emphasize individual letter differentiation in a sans-serif type face.

The type face also has an almost undistinguishable but effective tilt to the right, giving emphasis to that half of the letter which, research has shown, provides the best cues for recognition.

Space around individual letters needs to be proportional to the letter's width. Indiscriminate letter spacing does not increase legibility as such, Crosland and Johnson (31) showed. The legibility of typewriter letters, usually of uniform width, increased when spacing around the letters was proportional. This finding is particularly applicable to photo-typesetting machines based on the typewriter principle.

A typewriter face with standard space around the letters.

and customs to the c
structure is not nea

A new typewriter face with proportionally spaced letters, providing increased legibility.

progressive tax is o
increases; a regres

The variables influencing legibility of individual letters, then, are the complexity of letter outline, stroke width, heaviness, weight of hairlines, space within and around the letter, and differentiating letter features, Tinker (149) states.

Possibilities for a change in design of individual letters are now minimal for practical reasons. The need, however, for a more legible alphabet has been cited by a number of investigators such as Roethlein (116), Kolers (71), Sanford (118), Tinker (149), and others. That need remains. The topic will not be discussed here, however, since practical recommendations cannot be made. Some of the theoretical proposals by individual researchers and designers have been presented by Spencer (127) in detailed form.

Type size

Since one initial decision in typographic design concerns size of text type, it is not surprising that a large number of studies have investigated type sizes most beneficial to legibility.

A definition of the most legible type size has been hampered by the fact that x-heights for individual type faces differ greatly. Sizes of type faces come from the metal body on which the letter is cast, and which always must be accurate "to the point." Height of individual types faces on a uniform body (measured by the lower case "x" and therefore called "x-height") might vary considerably, and will in many cases. Some 8 point type faces may appear as large as a 10 point size of a different type design, while some 10 point type sizes may consist of a relatively small type design, giving it the appearance of a smaller size. Even small differences such as one point in type size significantly influence legibility of text type. (We are here primarily concerned with text type sizes in the neighborhood of 10 point, in which case a one point difference reflects 10% of the total size.)

With the trend toward photo-composition, for which the body-size/face-size problem is virtually non-existent, reclassification of type sizes seems to be necessary. Type sizes should eventually be determined by the x-height of the letters, and a uniform type size system should evolve, eliminating the problem caused by differing x-heights.

xh xh xh *xh*

Different type face samples, all of the same size (18 point), illustrating individual differences in x-height.

27

Research findings in optimal text type sizes have to be seen in light of the x-height problem. Paterson/Tinker (91, 93), and Tinker (135, 144) define the most legible type sizes to be either 9, 10, 11, or 12 point. The somewhat generous range of sizes stems from the differences in x-height. One carefully designed experiment by Poulton (110) avoided the x-height problem by matching type faces under investigation in actual x-height, reducing or enlarging different type faces so that they matched optically.

The experiment provided an interesting example of the problem: to achieve the same x-height (1.6 millimeters) for 2 type faces, Univers and Bembo, Univers had to be reduced to 9.5 point body size, while Bembo required a 12 point body size! In other words, a 2.5 point body size difference existed for 2 type faces of the same x-height.

A number of studies which have investigated the most legible text type sizes have produced results which support the Paterson/Tinker findings that 9, 10, 11, and 12 point provide for maximum legibility. Larger type sizes increase the number of fixations, since they take up more space both vertically and horizontally. Smaller type sizes simply reduce visibility of the type and hamper the all-important word recognition, Paterson/Tinker (92 and 99) showed. Larger sizes force readers to perceive words in sections, rather than as a whole, and consequently slow down reading speed, Tinker (136) found. In general, readers tend to prefer moderate type sizes and small amounts of leading, Hovde (64) reports.

While selecting type sizes for maximum legibility, distinction should be made between informative material requiring sustained reading, and referential text material of which only a small portion is to be read at a time. Adrian Frutiger, French typographer and designer, points out (49) that while maximum legibility must be desired for text requiring sustained reading, a different situation exists for referential material. Here considerations of space available seem to be of primary importance. Smaller type sizes than those of optimal legibility may be employed for such referential material. A combination of optimal and nonoptimal typography may provide best results in such cases.

■ **For text matter, a type size of 9, 10, 11, or 12 point should be selected. For type faces of a small x-height, 11 or 12 point should be used, while for type faces of a large x-height, a 9 or 10 point size might be most appropriate.**

Line width

Line width is another important contributor to legibility of continuously running text. Although it will be discussed as an independent factor for the time being, it is dependent on both type size and amount of leading, and, in a marginal context, on the type face selected.

For optimal type sizes of 9, 10, 11, and 12 point, about 10 to 12 words per line seem to be most comforting to the eye. That means in practical terms a line width of about 18 to 24 picas, depending on the letter width of the type face selected. Tinker/Paterson (160) determined the optimum line width for 10 point type to be 80 millimeters, which equals about 19 picas. In general, as reported by Paterson/Tinker (95, 96, 99) and Tinker (135, 141), a line width somewhere between 18 and 24 picas (for 10 point type) seems to be a safe guideline.

Less efficient reading will occur with very long and very short lines. Difficulties in reading short lines is contributed to an inability of the eye to make maximum use of horizontal perceptual cues. Difficult perception of very wide lines seems to come from inaccuracies and difficulties in relocating the beginning of each new line, Paterson/Tinker (96) report. The majority of readers found the most legible line width also to be most pleasing to the eye. In general, readers prefer a moderate line width.

Although smaller type sizes are less legible, they still have their optimal line widths. For 7 and 8 point, a line width of 12 picas produced greatest legibility, Tinker/Paterson (154) found.

■ **For optimal text sizes of 9, 10, 11, and 12 point, a line width of between 18 and 24 picas, consisting of about 10 to 12 words per line, should be selected.**

Leading

The third major factor contributing to legibility of text matter, the amount of leading, also has been investigated extensively.

The type face, of course, influences the amount of the leading necessary, and different type faces require varying amounts of leading, Becker et al. (11) found. Unleaded material is read relatively slowly, and reading rate increased with additional leading, Bentley (14) has shown. One experiment by Luckiesh/Moss (77), employing the eye blink technique, found the optimal amount of leading for 10 point size to be 3 point.

The optimal size of 10 point type, 19 picas wide (optimal width) seems to benefit most by 2 point leading, which increased reading speed by 7.5% over type set solid (no leading at all). An increase of leading to 4 points caused a 5% increase of reading speed, compared to solid type. For optimal sizes of 9, 10, 11, and 12 point, the most beneficial amount of leading ranges from 1 to 4 points, depending on the individual type face used, Paterson/Tinker (102) report.

■ For optimal type sizes of 9, 10, 11, and 12 point, the most
beneficial amount of leading for maximum legibility consists of
either 1, 2, 3, or 4 points. Judgment depends on the type face
used. Heavier type faces need more leading than light ones, but
all type faces are more legible with moderate leading than without
any at all.

Kinds of type

Before the words of an advertisement are read, the reader sees mere blocks of type. If that first visual impression does not intrigue him, he may never read those words you have so carefully chosen. Good

Before the words of an advertisement are read, the reader sees mere blocks of type. If that first visual impression does not intrigue him, he may never read those words you have so carefully cho-

Before the words of an advertisement are read, the reader sees mere blocks of type. If that first visual impression does not intrigue him, he may never read those words you have so careful-

Samples of light, medium, and bold versions of the same type face. The medium weight version is most legible.

Heaviness of individual letters provides another important clue to legibility. The ideal text type should be medium, not too heavy, and neither too light, Luckiesh and Moss (75) suggest. A type face too heavy (bold) tends to tire the eye easily. On the other hand, a type face of a very light design provides a rather poor differentiation from the paper background, and reduces legibility. The "brightness contrast," the perceived blackness of type against the brightness of the paper background, constitutes an important determinant of legibility, Tinker/Paterson (162) report.

Italic type, traditionally considered the superior mode of emphasis in text matter, actually is disliked by readers, Burt (23) and Paterson/Tinker (93) showed. Moreover, italics tend to slow down the reading speed, Tinker (145) found. Application of italics, when compared to roman, reduced reading speed by about 14 to 16 words per minute. Boldface, then, is more legible than italic, but it should be applied only in limited amounts, since it tires the eye easily.

■ For text matter, a type face of medium weight (not too light, not
too heavy) should be selected. For emphasis, bold face instead of
italic should be used in text matter. Bold face type should be used
sparingly, however, to avoid tiring of the eye.

A page from Gutenberg's 42-line Bible, with miraculously equalized word spacing.

Justified or unjustified typography?

One factor of typographic arrangement, unjustified typography compared to traditional justified (blocked-out) style, has been investigated often in recent years. In unjustified fashion, lines are set with a standardized word spacing, and no attempt is made to block out lines by adjusting word space. Lines are flush left, and excess space is added at the end of the line. In traditional, justified typography, lines are blocked out to a predetermined line width by adjusting (either enlarging or reducing) word space.

In general, there seems to be no significant difference in legibility of either justified or unjustified typography, a number of investigators showed. When 3 different right margins were investigated (unjustified, unjustified with a printed vertical guideline at the end, and justified), it was shown by Fabrizio et al. (42) that neither level of comprehension nor reading speed differed significantly for either one of the arrangements. In another case, investigated by Gregory/Poulton (54), no difference in reading speed or reader preference for either justified or unjustified composition was found.

In a similar study, unjustified lines, unjustified lines with a vertical line printed on the right, and justified lines were compared, and no practical difference between any of the arrangements, either in reading speed or level of comprehension, were found, Teal et al. (133) report.

In another study by Hartley/Burnhill (57), 3 different arrangements of unjustified typography were compared: (1) line endings determined by syntactic considerations (hyphenation was avoided where possible); (2) text with about ⅓ of the lines ending with hyphenated words; and (3) unjustified double column formats of different widths. Additionally, arrangements were compared with standard unjustified forms with line breaks determined by width of the line.

No significant differences in either one of these arrangements for reading speed or comprehension were found. There seemed to be a favorable attitude toward shorter lines with more uneven endings.

In another case, investigated by Wiggins (181), no difference in reading speed or reader preference for either justified or unjustified composition was found.

Gregory/Poulton (54) found that style of printing did not affect good readers, but poor readers read the justified, blocked-out text with considerably more difficulties.

A larger study by Davenport/Smith (33), investigating newspaper typography, found that justification of lines did not affect how accurately or quickly newspapers are read.

When the Dutch newspaper **Rotterdamsch Nieuwsblad** changed to unjustified typography for its entire production, there seemed to be little recognition of that change as such by the readership, Evers (41) reports. In an analysis of the typographic change, the paper found that production costs for unjustified typography were 13.5% lower than for justified typography. Additionally, there was no difference in the amount of printing (paper) space needed for either typographic form. Uniform word spacing in unjustified typography may also aid legibility, since adjustment to wide or narrow word space, necessary by the eye for justified typography, is not necessary.

A number of experiments, then, suggest that unjustified typography compares well to justified composition. There is some support that unjustified typography is actually preferred by readers. It takes up the same space as justified type, but reduces production costs. It will be less costly to make corrections on unjustified text matter: the ragged right-hand space may allow for a few more words to be added without resetting several lines, or a few words may be deleted by simply making the lines shorter, again without resetting much type that is so often necessary in justified style.

Groente-export vangt devaluatie pond zonder paniek op

ROTTERDAM — De devaluatie van het Engelse pond heeft de groenten- en fruitexport geen grote schade berokkend. Dit bleek vandaag uit mededelingen van exporteurs. Voor slechts een grote exportonderneming ligt de zaak slechter. Dit bedrijf zou voor meer dan 20.000 pond vorderingen in Engeland hebben uitstaan. Deze vorderingen verminderde het afgelopen weekeinde ruwweg met 28.000 gulden. Voor vele anderen echter betekent de devaluatie een onverwacht — tijdelijk — voordeeltje.

De meeste bedrijven leveren de Nederlandse tuinbouwprodukten aan hun Engelse afnemers op termijn. Deze bedrijven hadden al bij voorbaat hun ponden laten dekken. Hierdoor zijn leveringen die nog moeten plaatshebben in „zware" ponden betaald.

Het exportbedrijf Zwaan in Rotterdam heeft de zaak goed doorstaan. „Wanneer de devaluatie in de zomer was gekomen zou het harder zijn aangekomen". meende men. In de zomer zou men tevens de concurrentie van Spanje en de Canarische Eilanden moeten weerstaan. Zoals bekend heeft Spanje tegelijkertijd met Engeland zijn valuta gedevalueerd.

„Het zal wel een paar weken duren voordat men weer rust op de markt heeft", zei men ons bij de N. J. Mulder N.V. „Voorlopig is bijvoorbeeld de aanvoer van inlandse uien in Engeland groot genoeg voor de eigen consumptie. Tegen de helft van december heeft men hiervoor pas weer import nodig. De concurrentie van Spanje en de Canarische Eilanden is trouwens zeer betrekkelijk. Heel belangrijk is dat Nederland zijn havens het dichtst bij Engeland heeft", meende men.

„We verwachten geen rampzalige gevolgen. De prijs was toch al niet erg hoog en de meeste bedrijven hadden hun ponden gedekt. Tegen het begin van volgend jaar zullen de prijzen zich waarschijnlijk weer op een reëel niveau gestabiliseerd hebben. Tegen die tijd is ook de eigen Engelse produktie ongeveer verkocht", zei men bij Jac. van As N.V.

De exporteurs zijn in elk geval door de devaluatie niet uit het veld geslagen. „Veel collega's hebben de bui zien hangen en hebben van tevoren al maatregelen getroffen", zei men op de veiling Noord.

Veiling Berkel en Rodenrijs

VEILING BERKEL EN RODENRIJS, RODENRIJS, 21 nov. : glassla I 12 19.00; II 9.50—13.50, C 8.00; tomaten 7.00—7.30, B 6.30, C 5.50—5.70; toma A-B'land 2.40—2.50, B 3.20; spruiten Heden werden aangevoerd 7000 kg maten en 134.000 st glassla.

DE PLOEG van het extra-sportieve merk Smiths voor het seizoen 1967 i volgt samengesteld: Planckaert, Va den Berghe, Van Vlierberghe, De B ver, Van de Rysse, Brusselmans, De Sweeveld, Claes, Brands, Monty (al België), Dolman, Zoet, Duyndam, B wer, Heynig, Du Bois en Hoogerlan (allen Nederland).

Verzoek aan min

Verolme v arbeiders

ROTTERDAM — Verolm heeft minister Roolvink (so le zaken) toestemming gevraagd om driehonderd Spa se werknemers aan te trekk

De bewindsman heeft nog geen beslissing genomen.

Uit het verzoek blijkt, dat d wervingsactie voor nieuw pers neel tot nu toe niet het gewer resultaat hebben gehad.

Volgens het ministerie doen van bedrijven nog regelmati een beroep op buitenlandse a

SCHEEPVAART

ROTTERDAM AANGEKOMEN 21 NOVEMBER
VESTEROY, Noor, Br. Columbia, Maashaven, N.Z., pulp, Furness
KYLIX, Ned., Thameshaven, Shell 32, ledig, Van Ommeren
UNIKASS, Dts., Bergen, Koningin Wilhelminahaven Vlaardingen, olie, Furness
KULMERLAND, Dts., Marseille, Merwehaven, pier 6, stg., PHM
HEINZ HORN, Dts., Kingslijn, Beatrixhaven ledig, Muller
WAKEFIELD, Eng., Hull, Beatrixhaven, stg., Humber Diensten
ESTRELLA, Noor, Santos, 2e Eemhaven stg., Burger
VINDICAT, Ned., Split, Westerkade, erts, Erh. & Dekkers
ESSO FLAME, Fin., Petit Couronne, Esso Botlek, ledig, Esso Nederland
ESSO YORK, Eng., La Salina, Che-

2de Pethaven, Chevron, ldg, Muller
BISMARCKSTEIN, Dts., Londen, Spoorhaven, stg., Sanara
STEINHOFT, Dts., Antw., Beatrixhaven, stg., James Smith
SCHOONEBEEK, Ned., Rauma, Rijnhaven, Molukken, stg., Spliethoff
BARGUZIN, Rus. Kaliingrad, Maashaven, pier 6, stg., PHM
NORWIND, Ned., Hull, Benaluxhaven, stg., Noordzee Veerdiensten
SPIRALITY, Eng., Colchester, Parkkade, ldg, Wagenborg
DORIS, Dts., Hamburg, Zwijndrecht, olie, Alg. Vrachtk.
EVA, Noor, Sauda, Waalhaven, pier 5, Ned. Rijnv. Veren.
CAPACITY, Eng., Felixstowe, Binnenhaven, stg., Trias
HERMANN LITMEYER, Dts., Lowestoft, Merwehaven, stg., Ker-

ISIS Ned Londen
AFOUNDRIA Am Bremen
POOL FISHER Eng Felixstowe
ELSA ESSBERGER Dts Bremerhaven

VERTROKKEN 22 NOVEMBER
ANDROMEDA, Ned., Mostaganem
PORTRIEUX, Frans. Klaipeda
CRESTA, Ned., Goole
NICOLE, Ned., Waterford
OELTANK 1, Dts., Hamburg
SEESCHWALBE, Dts., Drogheda
BRITTENBURGH, Ned., Newcastle
EASTWOOD, Eng., Hull
KRAFTCA, Ned., Hamburg
NORGIT, Frans, Port Jerome
KORALLE, Dts., Hango
BITUMA, Deen. Kopenhagen
TANK DUCHESS, Noor, Falmouth
JOHN HELLESKOV, Deen, Vaste
GRETKE OLDENDORFF, Dts..
Rostock
WINERTOR, Dts., Emden
ESSO FLAME, Fin., Fawley
STOLT AVENIR, Ital., Aarhus
ANVERS, Belg, Antw.
DEBEN, Eng., Londen
NAGASAKI, Zw., Penang
GREGERSO, Fin., Bathurst
HINNITES, Eng., Thameshaven
DIONE, Frans, Caen
ORNEFJELL, Noor. Antw.
WIASMA, Rus. Antw.

Bianca 22 te Ipswich ver
Bilitar 21 70 m OZO E. L
Boekanier 22 te Londen
Bonafide 20 te Rochester
Bontekoe 21 175 m WZV
Bontekoning 23 te Sunda
Boreas 21 v Malaga te C
Borelly 21 v Deltzijl n Si
Borneo 21 op 60 m W R
Bornrif 22 te Honfleur v
Botlania 21 v Umea n Do
Bovenkerk 21 420 m ON
na
Biscajaris 22 te Hamburg
Breewijk p 21 IJmuiden
burg
Brinoa 22 te IJmuiden
Brinio 21 te Helsingborg
Br. um 21 360 m O Mi
folk
Brittenburgh 22 v Rott n

Codans 22 te Londen
Cidamares 21 v feie n Ci
Cameroenkust 22 te King
Capricornus 22 te Lissab
Caronan 20 v Leixoes n C
Carebeka 2, 21 v Yarmou
Hartkepcol
Carebeka 4 p 22 K. Penz
Cartago 21 op 480 m NV
Castor 22 te Antw.
Cdstali 22 v Boston n Bre
Catharina 23 te Leixoes
Catharina F 20 te Oxelos
Ceres 21 v La Guaira n

The Dutch newspaper after it changed to unjustified typography.

34

Finally, unjustified style will eliminate much of the problem caused with hyphenation in computerized typesetting by avoiding the breaking of words from one line to the next.

■ **Application of unjustified typography is recommended on the basis of extensive research findings which did not discover significant differences in legibility between justified and unjustified composition. Unjustified typography reduces production costs, possibly aids legibility, makes for an easier correction procedure, and provides a contemporary, relaxed typographic style.**

Lowercase or uppercase typography?

Outline-shape, unique for each word in lower-case letters.

Outline-shape, uniform for words set in all-caps.

Words are perceived by their specific word-shape outline, which is unique for lowercase words. Once the outline of the word has been perceived and stored in memory, future recognition or recall of the word takes place without letter-by-letter deciphering. Words set in all-caps, however, do not provide specific word-shape outlines since they produce an oblong, uniform word-shape. No cues can be perceived by the eye, and a time-consuming deciphering of the word, letter by letter, is necessary. Further evidence for this process was supplied by Tinker (148) when he found that more reading errors were made in reading lowercase words than of words set in all-caps, indicating that all-caps words are indeed read letter by letter, while lowercase words are not.

Words set in all caps use up to 30% more space than words set in lower case, Tinker/Paterson (156) found, which leads to an increase in time-consuming eye fixations, 4.74 words per second, the study showed, can be read in all-caps type, and 5.38 words per second can be read in lowercase type.

Text set in all-caps retards reading speed by about 13%, due to an increase in fixation time, and a corresponding decrease in the number of words perceived per fixation, Tinker/Paterson (98 and 155) showed.

Words are perceived by their specific outline shape

WORDS ARE PERCEIVED BY THEIR SPECIFIC OUTLINE SHAPE

Words are perceived by their specific outline shape

An illustration of additional space necessary for all-caps typography: the sentence in all-caps takes up considerably more space than a lowercase line in the same type size. A much larger type size may be used instead, occupying the same amount of horizontal space, but more effectively.

Application of all-caps typography in single column newspaper headlines also reduces reading speed by about 19%, according to Breland (19). However, no difference in legibility has been found between headlines set in all lowercase, and those with only the first letter of the word in caps, Hvistendahl (67) reports.

■ **Wherever possible, the usage of type set in all-caps should be avoided. For emphasis, bold face or a larger type face should be used instead.**

Alternatives: spaced-unit, square-unit

For a considerable time there has been discussion about the best presentation of textual matter in typography. Can a better arrangement than the long, horizontal line be found? Proposals have centered around presentation of text matter in space-units, square-units, and several "chunk" variations.

Spaced-unit style breaks sentences into meaningful thought units by adding additional space between these units for better reading differentiation.

This is	**an example**	**of such a**	**spaced-unit form.**

Square-units break sentences down into thought patterns too, but present them in double-line arrangement.

This is	**of the application**	**in straight**
an example	**of a square-unit**	**matter text.**

It seems that presentation of technical training material into square-span and spaced-unit style may present certain advantages over the traditional arrangements, as reported by Klare et al. (70). They found square-span initially slowed down the reading process, but with practice the retarded reading tended to diminish. Arrangement in spaced-unit forms had little effect on reading speed. When the "thought units" were smaller, rather than larger, the new arrangements were found more acceptable to the reader. One advantage was that the new arrangement led to increased testing scores for the better readers.

A "vertical" typography, consisting of very short lines, with the main reading direction vertically, and consisting of several columns per page, has been proposed by W. S. Brown (21). Suggesting that this arrangement makes reading faster, easier, and more reliable, he proposed that computers be used to prepare the text for this particular typographic arrangement.

A sample of "vertical" typography, proposed by Brown.

Most normal readers move their eyes across the page from left to right once for each line of text. In this mode the brain is sometimes able to process the information more rapidly than the eyes are able to transmit it. As a result the mind may wander, and there may be a significant loss of comprehension.

The key to speed-reading, as taught in certain popular courses, is to take in several lines of text during each pass across the page. When this is done, the words are not transmitted in the proper order, and therefore the brain must either rearrange them or understand them out of order. To achieve still greater speed, the eyes pass from left to right with a downward slope, and the omitted regions are picked up on the return. Normal readers who receive training in speed-reading are often able to improve their reading speeds by factors of four or five, with equal or greater comprehension.

Poulton[1] contends that speed-reading is accomplished not by storing information

One study by North and Jenkins (88), comparing reading speed for standard arrangements, spaced-unit style, and square-unit style, reports the square-unit style to be superior to other styles investigated.

For long passages of text, Coleman and Kim (30) found, the conventional arrangement was read faster than all other styles, while, when the tachistoscope was used, the new style vertical, spaced-unit, and square-span were superior to the traditional arrangement.

In another experiment by Nashinsky (86), the square-span style produced comprehension scores quite superior to both spaced-unit style and the traditional horizontal line arrangement. It is suggested that the square-span style may lead to increased reading speed and comprehension.

A study by Carver (26) failed to discover significant differences between chunked formats and the traditional forms of typography.

By and large, then, research investigating composition of text matter into smaller units has not provided strong conclusive findings. But neither has it been shown that they are detrimental to legibility. Perhaps a careful, selective application of some of these new styles, on an experimental basis, might provide some feedback.

★ **On the basis of investigations, which, however, were not very conclusive, it is proposed that square-unit style and spaced-unit style be applied in selected cases and on an experimental basis. Reader response might be favorable after an initial exposure time, and reading and comprehension speed might be improved. The methods, it seems, might best be applied in the typography of educational material, and in display advertising.**

Ligatures and legibility

Ligatures can be another important determinant of legibility. Gutenberg, in his first major work, the 42-line Bible, had more than 290 characters, ligatures, and abbreviations available to aid him in achieving beautifully blocked out lines, Zapf (184) reports.

Storage problems (in typecases and magazines), deriving from the application of ligatures in metal typesetting, have reduced usage of ligatures. With computerized photo-composition, however, technical obstacles in ligature applications have largely disappeared.

Scorsone (121) designed a system of 17 ligatures as an addition to both a sans-serif and a roman font. Since word shape, elementary to word recognition, will be narrowed with the help of special ligatures, more letters and/or words may be perceived within one normal fixation pause.

an ar as be de
ec ed ee em en er
ff is it ns oo

Ligatures designed by Scorsone for Century Schoolbook type.

Typography is the art of visual communication. It has one fundamental duty before it and that is to transmit ideas in writing. No argument or consideration can absolve typography from this duty. A printed work that cannot be read becomes a product without purpose. - Emil Ruder

The ligatures applied in regular text matter.

A line set with special ligatures (above) compared to one set by regular metal type, illustrating the reduction of word width.

The return of the ligature
The return of the ligature

Since the eye span in reading normally covers about 2 centimeters, special ligatures allow the eye to perceive more letters within one normal eye span, a factor which should help increase reading speed. Erdman and Neal (40) have shown that familiar words are perceived almost as quickly as individual letters, reinforcing the finding that word outline elicits meaning rather than a deciphering of the word. A temporary learning process, however, familiarizing the reader with new ligature symbols, might be necessary, but seems to be justified by the eventual gain in reading time.

★ **In photo-typesetting, the design and usage of special ligatures is encouraged. Particularly in headline and display typography, "close" typesetting, resulting in overlapping and touching of individual letters, may result in increased perception per fixation pause and greater reading speed.**

Television typography

In general, legibility research concerns itself with printed type on paper. But new problems of typographic legibility arise with the application of type to the electronic media, television.

Typical blurring and distortion of letters on a TV screen.

Problems of type distortion and decay unknown to print medium are common to type display on television. Type on the television screen tends to fill in easily, sharp corners tend to become rounded, and fine serifs tend to disappear completely. The use of type faces with thin strokes on television should therefore be restricted.

The new type face, CBS News 36, designed especially for the TV screen.

A new type face, CBS News 36, designed especially for use on TV by Bass (9), attempts to eliminate or at least to reduce some of the problems caused by the television screen. Another new TV type face, the Lincoln/MITRE font, failed to produce significant improvement in television legibility, but valuable insights into television type designs were gained, Bass (10) reports.

★ **For television typography, sans-serif type faces of medium weight or serif type faces without thin, sharp serifs should be used.**

Numbers

A surprisingly large amount of research has gone into the legibility of numerals, mathematical symbols, and the arrangement of mathematical tables.

2314

two-thousand-three-
hundred-and-fourteen

Arabic numerals take up less space and are
more quickly perceived (fewer fixation pauses),
than numerals in word form.

1967 1967

Old Style numerals (left), with differentiating
descenders, are more legible than numerals in
Modern Roman (right).

Numbers in the form of Arabic numerals are read faster and with fewer fixations than numbers written out in word form, Tinker (143) reports. Although numbers as such are read more slowly than individual letters, when perceived as a group they are comprehended faster than words. Arabic numerals not only have a more compact form, but also favor reading speed. For instance, "2314" is easier to perceive in numerals than "two-thousand-three-hundred-and-fourteen." Numerals also take up less space.

Arabic numerals, when compared to Roman numerals, are read faster in all reading conditions, Perry (108) found. This seems to be caused by both the greater differentiation of Arabic numerals and the relative familiarity of the reader with Arabic symbols.

Old Style numerals, with differentiating ascenders and descenders, are somewhat more legible than Modern numerals when işolated, and considerably more legible when in groups, Tinker (150) discovered. The greater differentiation of the Old Style numerals accounts for the difference here.

● **Numbers should be set in Arabic numerals, not in word form. Arabic numerals should be used instead of Roman numerals. Old Style numerals are more readable than Modern Roman numerals, and should be used where possible, particularly in headline and display typography.**

Mathematical material

A number of studies have investigated legibility of mathematical tables. When Frase (48) compared tabular presentation with diagrammic presentations, he found that diagrams were the superior learning device. However, arrangement and presentation in tabular form was preferred by the readers.

Grouping of numerals in vertical groups of 5 greatly helped the locating of items in a table and promoted legibility, Tinker (140) reports. About one pica space or one pica space with a rule was equally effective in separating columns of numerals.

The type size for tabular matter should be at least 8 point. Tables should not be too wide nor crowded by an excessive number of columns. There should be generous leading, and the items in the first column are best set in bold face type, Tinker (146) reports.

● **When learning is the major concern, diagrammic presentation should be used, and, when reader preference is taken into consideration, tabular presentation should be selected. Tables should be set in at least 8 point type, with generous leading. The material should be broken into vertical groups of five, with the first column in bold face, and at least one pica space and/or rule between the columns. Tables should not be too long and not be crowded by too many columns.**

Color and background

A related problem in typographic design concerns paper color and background. The problem has been investigated by a number of researchers, and relatively similar results have been reported.

The brightness contrast between print and background seems to be the most important factor when color in printing is under consideration, Tinker/Paterson (162) have shown.

Two studies by Hackman/Tinker (56), and Tinker/Paterson (162) tried to determine the most efficient color combination for print on paper. Black on white, and black on yellow seem to provide best legibility results, both studies showed. Similarly, both investigations emphasize again brightness contrast as a major factor in determining the color/paper combination for maximum legibility.

Individual differences in the surface of printing paper have been investigated by several researchers, including Luckiesh/Moss (80), Stanton/Burtt (128), and Webster/Tinker (175). All report that, with the possible exception of extreme "whiteness," which seems to advance legibility, paper surface has little influence on legibility.

● **Selection of paper and color of ink should be directed toward achieving a maximum "brightness contrast."**

Type in reverse

Type in reverse, that is, white type on dark or black background, retards reading, several studies have proven. When 10 point text type in reverse (white on black) was tested against the normal black-on-white arrangement, Holmes (62) found the reverse arrangement retarded reading speed by 14.7%.

In another study, investigating the same problem, Paterson/Tinker (101) found black-on-white printing to be 10.5% superior in reading speed to the white-on-black arrangement. It was suggested that when reversed type is being used to attract attention, it should be restricted to very small amounts of copy, and to type sizes of at least 10 or 12 point. A retardation of reading speed and legibility for white print on black background is also reported by Taylor (131).

Reversed type is also least preferred by readers: 77.7% in a study by Paterson/Tinker (101) found the black-on-white arrangement more pleasing to the eye.

■ **Type in reverse (white on black) should be avoided for small type sizes, and used sparingly for larger type.**

Sound units in a second color

A recent study by Hinds/Dodds (60) has shown that the learning process in elementary reading can be improved by employing color selected sounds units. In a learning situation for beginning readers, selected similar sound units (i.e., **two**, w**oo**, dr**ew**), were printed in a second color. For both primary-school children and inner-city illiterate adults, superior vocabulary and comprehension gains were achieved for the 2 color group when compared to the group using identical text but printed in black only. Additionally, better reading was attained with one-color books after pupils had initially been introduced to reading with the 2 color approach.

★ **In elementary reading learning situations, selected application of color for sound units is encouraged. It is suggested that the Hinds/Dodds study is consulted for details.**

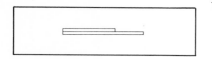

The number and varieties of line widths in the original design.

The number and varieties of line widths in the new design.

Simplification of design units

A proposal by Bonsiepe (18) promises to both reduce the order of technical arrangement (by reducing the number of typographic elements used), and to improve the optical appearance of the design by such technical simplification. An old piece of ephemera was redesigned, resulting in a reduced number of typographic elements, such as line width, type sizes, and leading.

★ **For production and design simplification, the smallest number possible of line widths and spacing units, as shown by Bonsiepe, should be employed.**

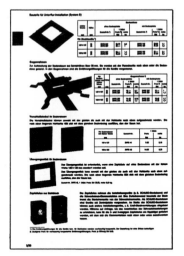
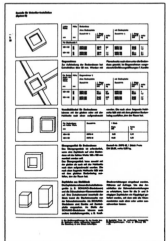

The original design.   The redesign, with only 2 basic line widths.

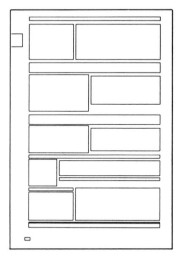
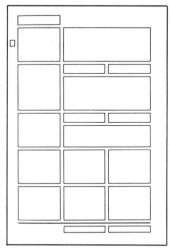

Outlines of graphic units, the original   Outlines of graphic units, the redesign
version.   version.

Unit spacing

A promising proposal for arrangement of horizontal spacing based on a uniform proportional method has been made by P. Burnhill (22). The system categorizes the horizontal units of space on a page, based on a simple proportional system, and then assigns these predetermined spatial units to the pages. Proportional amounts of space are assigned to paragraphs, above and below headings (which are broken into ranks of first, second, and third order, and so on). A paragraph, for instance, may be signalled by one preceding space unit. A third order headline may be assigned two units above, one unit below, and so on. The proportional system can be based on simply doubling the spatial units, such as 1:2:4:8, or any proportional system may be applied. The proposal seems to be particuarly valuable to application in computerized typesetting, where uniform spatial units can be easily programmed into the typesetting process. A substantial saving in pasteup time as well as an orderly aesthetic appearance of the page may result from such a proportional spatial system.

★ **Particularly for application in computerized typesetting, a comprehensive, predetermined system of horizontal spacing, based on proportional units, is seen to be beneficial to both economy of production, and improvement of design arrangement in general.**

Legibility of children's books

Are larger-than-standard type sizes necessary in printing schoolbooks for the primary grades? When the effects of type size and various factors such as mental age, intelligence, etc., were investigated, all groups of children read standard type sizes faster than the larger ones, Alderman (1) found. The practice of printing text books for primary grades in larger-than-normal type sizes may therefore not be necessary. Type size in general, it has been found by Gilliland (51), is not as decisive an influence on the reading habits of children as has been traditionally assumed.

Tinker (135) concludes that from the 5th grade on, type sizes proven to be most legible to adult readers may be used for children's books.

● **Optimal type sizes (9, 10, 11, 12 point) may be employed for children's books, beginning with the 5th grade, without creating reading difficulties.**

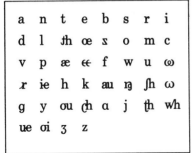

An i.t.a. alphabet application to the Century Schoolbook type face.

The Initial Teaching Alphabet

In teaching elementary reading, the Initial Teaching Alphabet (i.t.a.) is finding growing application. The use of i.t.a. in schoolbook printing has been handicapped by lack of adequate type characters specific to the alphabet. A number of type faces such as Century Schoolbook, Baskerville, Melior, Helvetica, and Optima have now had special i.t.a. characters designed for their fonts by Montague (84).

★ **For texts using the i.t.a, one of the type faces with specially designed i.t.a. characters should be used.**

49

Miscellaneous findings

A variety of individual research findings will be presented here. All of them may contribute to a functional typography. Most of the findings are of a minute nature, but good typography consists of a conglomerate of many small design decisions.

One-column or double-column arrangement?

When legibility and reader preference of single column and double column typography was compared, Foster (46) found that the arrangement employing 2 columns of 17 picas was read faster than when the same text was arranged in one column of 32 picas width. This finding is partly supported by the results on maximum line width presented earlier.

● **Double-column arrangement, consisting of a maximum line width, should be used instead of long-line, single-column arrangement.**

Medley typography or plain style?

A fine balance exists between an interesting, appealing typographic arrangement and one that is overloaded and has the reverse effect. When reading values of 2 medley typographic arrangements were compared with one consisting of straight, regular text, Tinker/Paterson (157) found that the medley arrangement retarded reading speed by 8.35% and 11.39% respectively. However, medley arrangements were found to be more pleasing to the eye. Apparently a medley arrangement should be applied when attention is sought, while, when legibility is the main consideration, as few type faces and type sizes as possible should be used. Undesirable typographic arrangements, Paterson/Tinker (91) have shown, tend to operate together to decrease typographic legibility considerably.

● **For attention value, a modest medley arrangement elicits pleasant reader response. When legibility is of main concern, medley style should be avoided since it decreases reading speed.**

Indentions

Tinker/Paterson (93) found that a moderate indention at the beginning of a paragraph improves reading speed by about 7%. For design of this booklet, however, additional horizontal space (one unit) between paragraphs has been selected in place of indentions.

● **A moderate indention (about 2 or 3 ems) increases reading speed and should be used. It is felt, however, that additional leading may be equally adequate.**

Value of white space

Traditionally, white space in generous proportions has been considered an important and valuable factor in typographic design. Strong (129), investigating the value of additional white space in advertising, reports that additional white space considerably increased the attention value of ads. In financial terms, increased costs for additional advertising space are upset by elevated attention value of the ad, attracting more readers. A reported limit of an additional 60% spacial increase, which would justify the increased placement costs in comparison to the increased attention elicited, has to be seen in light of prevailing advertising costs in 1926, the year the study was conducted.

● **Generous proportions of white space in advertisements should be applied to secure the attention value of the ad.**

All-display typography

Recent years have brought increased all-display typography in advertising. A study by Turnbull and Carter (169) came to the conclusion that all-display typography in advertising (type sizes much larger than necessary for maximum legibility) is not restrictive in attracting reader attention and interest. However, the effect on the readership beyond the reader-interest level was not seen to be high. In other words, no significant gains in attention value are reported from all-display typography.

● **All-display typography may be applied for advertisements without significantly influencing the attention value.**

Headline sizes

Different headline type faces vary in the degree of their legibility, English (38) observed. Sizes between 14 and 30 point, in general, are equally legible. Newspaper text type, by and large, is more difficult to read than comparable text type in book printing, Paterson/Tinker (106) showed. The difference is attributed to the

An all-display advertisement from the Turnbull/Carter study.

relative grayness of the newspaper stock, as compared to the relative whiteness of book paper. The "brightness-contrast" factor, mentioned earlier, influences the perception of the printed word.

● **For newspaper headlines, type sizes from 14 to 30 point may be applied with equally good results.**

Newspaper front pages

The makeup of the front pages of newspapers, research by Click and Stempel (28) suggests, influences the judgment readers may make about the entire newspaper. In general, respondents seem to prefer horizontal pages and dislike symmetric makeup.

● **Horizontal front page makeup for newspapers is recommended.**

Calligraphy

Manuscript writing, the art of calligraphy, usually finds application in printing only in selected cases. Calligraphy is more difficult to read than typewritten, handwritten, or typeset text, Bell (12, 13) reports. Where maximum legibility is concerned, calligraphy should not be used. However, most print application of calligraphy is not concerned with reading speed, and legibility findings are of marginal nature for this beautiful typographic art form.

● **When reading speed is of consideration, calligraphy should be used only in small amounts.**

The Lord is my shepherd;
I shall not want. He maketh me
to lie down in green pastures;
he leadeth me beside the still waters.
He restoreth my soul;
he leadeth me in the paths
of righteousness for his name's sake.
Yea, though I walk through
the valley of the shadow of death,
I will fear no evil: for thou art with me;
thy rod and thy staff they comfort me.
Thou preparest a table before me
in the presence of mine enemies:
thou anointest my head with oil;
my cup runneth over.
Surely goodness and mercy
shall follow me all the days of my life
and I will dwell in the house
of the Lord forever. Psalm 23

A fine example of calligraphy by G. Harvey Petty.

Backbone titles

Backbone titles for books were found to be more readable when printed in a downward direction, providing for better word recognition, a study by Burt et al. (25) suggests.

- **Backbone titles should be printed in a downward direction.**

Inner margins

The inner margins in bound publications and books may influence significantly legibility, Tinker (139) found. Curving of the text, caused by small inner margins, significantly reduced reading rate and visibility of words.

- **Inner margins should be wide enough to prevent curving of the text matter.**

Congeniality

The concept of congeniality or atmosphere-value of printing type has been investigated by several researchers. They have, however, restricted themselves to investigating different possibilities and values of congeniality studies. Generally, there is good reason to assume some of the methods of investigation will eventually produce valuable research results in this important field of type face "expression." Until now, however, studies conducted are primarily of an exploratory nature.

abcdefghij vwxyzäöü

ABCDEFG PQRRSTU

abcdefghijklm
äöüßßb&
ABCDEFG
NOPQRS
AOUTh

abcdefghijkln
äöüchckßß&
ABCDEFGH
STUVWXYZ

abcdefghijkln
äöüchckß&
ABCDEFGH
STUVWXYZ

Some of the type faces tested by Wendt for congeniality or atmosphere-value.

In a study by Tannenbaum et al. (132), it was established that typography may communicate connotative variations. It is concluded that, despite some notable problems, there seems to be substantial basis for the use of typography as a code for the communication of connotative variations.

Another study by Kastl/Child (69), investigating the influence of type face variables on the judgment of emotional meaning, found that specific type faces tend to express specific moods.

The semantic differential, a scaling technique using standardized descriptions for various kinds of objects, was used in a study by Wendt (180). While the results of the study as such, the "atmosphere-value" of certain type faces, ought to be interpreted cautiously, it was shown that this specific technique of investigation may be applied with good results.

The semantic scale used by Wendt to test the congeniality of type faces (partial).

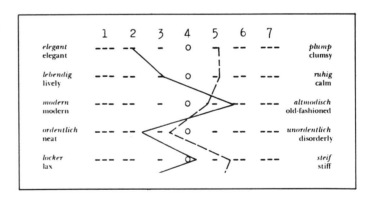

By and large, research into congeniality of type faces is at an initial stage. Results of investigations have only shown the value of certain methods of investigation. Eventually, however, results from careful investigations into the congeniality of type faces may become an important determinant in the selection of type faces for typographic design.

55

The following are a number of findings, which, while not suitable for recommendations, may provide the typographer with better understanding of certain legibility factors.

The part-whole illusion

In many cases, reader's proportional perception of white space and print suffers from the part-whole illusion, Paterson/Tinker (105) showed. For the normal book page, the relationship of printed area to white surrounding space is about 50:50. However, the study showed readers believe 75% of the page to be covered by print.

Telephone directory style

Maximum legibility for typography of telephone directory was determined in another study by Baird (4). A 4-column arrangement with one point leading in 6 point type was found to be most legible. The findings were consequently applied to the New York telephone directory.

The amount of text read

How much of the text in an ad is read by the average reader? Dulsky (36) investigated how much of the copy in magazine advertisements was read. The average person, the study found, spends about 10 seconds looking at the copy of an ad and reads about 5% to 10% of it. For the more wordy ads, there was a

An example of the part-whole proportional illusion: both black and white area cover about 50% of the page, although visually the black area seems to be larger.

tendency for a smaller percentage of the copy to be read. Finally, there was a marked tendency to read more copy on the left-hand pages.

"Good" versus "poor" typography

One extensive experiment by Wrolstad (182) tested the level of agreement on "good" typography as experts saw it, and the way unbiased individuals perceived it. By and large, there was significant agreement of both groups on samples of "good" typography. More symmetric than asymmetric typographic arrangements were selected, and — young women seem to be more appreciative of "good" typography than young men.

Legibility and pleasingness correlate

Correlation of perceived good legibility and perceived pleasingness of a typographic arrangement, mentioned earlier, was specifically investigated in an experiment by Tinker/Paterson (158), and close agreement between these two factors was found.

Dictionary typography

Glanville et al. (52) report that for dictionary typography, the main words were located more easily, and the arrangement was preferred by readers (both children and adults) when set in 12 point type, as compared to an arrangement using 6 point type for main words. 12 point type for only main words provides maximum efficiency in locating items, while the referential text material, in 6 point, takes into account spatial limitations of dictionary typography.

Fatigue in reading

For how long can the eye go on reading without any tiring effect? If there is fatigue after prolonged reading, what factors cause or influence such fatigue?

Under optimal reading conditions, and when the context of the reading material is of general interest to the reader, prolonged reading for many hours without signs of fatigue can be maintained. When reading of books and of microfilm material was compared, no evidence of fatigue for either group was found after 2 hours of reading, although the microfilm material was read more rapidly without surrounding light, Anderson and Meredith (2) report.

When fatigue in reading does occur, it results in an increased number of fixations per line, slower reading rate, more regressions, reduced accuracy of perception, and weakened comprehension, Demilia (34) found. Typographic variables, improving legibility in general, may successfully battle reading fatigue, but context of the material remains an equally important determinant.

4 Research applications in design and production of booklet

For the design and production of this booklet, as many research recommendations and proposals as possible were applied. Similarly, typographic practices shown to diminish legibility were avoided.

The type

The text type has been set by Linofilm. Selection of a medium weight type face, Palatino Roman, in 9 point size with 3 point leading, 23 picas basic width, reflects research findings in type weight, size, leading, and line width. Subheads were set in 11 point Helvetica Bold Roman. Chapter heads are in 16 point Helvetica Roman. For emphasis in text matter, bold face was selected, instead of italics, which has been shown to hamper legibility. Captions were set in 7 point Helvetica Roman. The bibliography, consisting of referential material, has been set in a size slightly below the maximum legibility level, in 8 point Palatino Roman with Bold, following Frutiger's recommendation (49).

The Palatino type face is a creation of German type designer Hermann Zapf. Helvetica was designed by Max Miedlinger of Switzerland.

All type has been set in unjustified style, which simplifies the typesetting process, and should result in increased legibility over the blocked-out traditional style. Consequently, the text appears without wordbreaking hyphenation. All-caps typography has also been avoided, except in cases where abbreviations (i.e., MITRE) were concerned.

All type has been set "closely" (a process easily available on photo-typesetting equipment) to narrow word width and increase perception range. Numbers, as suggested by research, are usually set in Arabic numerals, not in word form.

The design approach

Design and arrangement of pages is based on a grid system consisting of one-pica squares. Since the text type was set in 9 on 12 point (one pica per line), a convenient system of working units was established. There are only 2 line widths, 23 pica for text matter, and 12 pica for captions, reflecting Bonsiepe's proposal on reduction of typographic elements used (18). For the horizontal space distribution, the unit spacing proposal by Burnhill (22) has been applied.

All spacing consists of one-pica units, conforming to the grid system used. There are 3 units above subheads, 2 units below, and one unit between paragraphs. 2 space units were placed above and below illustrations in the text column. On occasion pages run short to avoid a bad line break.

Indentions, although shown to increase reading speed, were not used since additional space between paragraphs, employed here, serves the same purpose. The inner margins of the pages are wider than established traditionally to avoid curving of the text which may reduce reading rate.

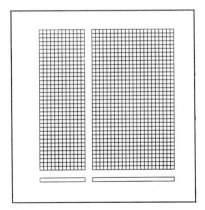

The grid system used for the production of this booklet (reduced). All units are one-pica squares.

60

Conclusion and outlook

In what direction should legibility research and application of research findings go?

First of all, univariate research, that is, investigation of individual typographic variables, should be increased and broadened. These individual research findings are the particles of the mosaic that makes for better legibility.

Secondly, the interaction of various legibility findings needs to be investigated on a broader scale. Perhaps a comparative testing of several applied research findings with an arrangement using random typographic elements may present the most valuable results.

Thirdly, all the methods of measuring legibility still remain in need of improvement. Methods of subject selection and pre-screening, and a tight experimental control of the experimental situation are perhaps the major factors in need of refinement.

Lastly, coordination and accumulation of legibility research on an international basis is needed: legibility research today not only flourishes in such Western countries as England, Sweden, the United States, and West Germany, but is also being emphasized in Czechoslovakia, East Germany, Poland, and Russia. The formation of the **International Committee on Legibility Research,** and the appearance of publications such as **Legibility Research Abstracts** and **Visible Language** will aid the accumulation of all legibility research conducted.

In a related context, the appearance of computerized reading machines will have to be taken under consideration. Not only human perception of typography, but also the requirements of reading machines need to concern the typographer.

Furthermore, typographic legibility plays an increasingly important role in such media as television, film, microfilm audio-visual learning devices, and others. The specific technical-typographical requirements of these message carriers need to be investigated.

The research findings presented in this project as recommendations are, in general, well supported by a number of research findings — but are also few in numbers. The proposals are based on one or more studies and on the subjective judgment of this researcher. A reasonable case for their application can be made, but individual judgments, influenced by the specific typographic situation, will be necessary.

While a conscientious attempt has been made to accumulate all research in legibility conducted so far, it is realized that some significant studies may have escaped the attention of this researcher. But it is felt that with the accumulation, evaluation, and selection of practically applicable research findings, and with the formation of recommendations and proposals, the groundwork has been laid for a more functional typography, a typography based on scientific legibility research.

This attempt, it is hoped, will initiate and aid future efforts in the important field of typographic communications.

Credits

Publications with emphasis on legibility research

icographic, A quarterly Review of International Visual Communication Design. Published quarterly by The International Council of Graphic Design Associations, 7 Templeton Court, Radnor Walk, Shirley Croydon CRO 7NZ, England.

Visible Language, The Journal for Research on the Visual Media of Language Expression (formerly **The Journal of Typographic Research**). Published quarterly by Merald E. Wrolstad, Ph.D., Editor and Publisher, % The Cleveland Museum of Art, Cleveland, Ohio 44106.

Glossary

Brightness contrast	Relationship between "blackness" of type and "whiteness" of paper.
Congeniality	Emotional connotation or "atmosphere-value" of type.
Fixation	Pause of the eye during reading sweep, when actual perception of words takes place.
Ligature	A combination of 2 or more letters in one character unit.
Medley typography	A variety of typographic elements (type faces, sizes, etc.) combined.
Modern Roman	Type face with straight, thin serifs, usually no descenders or ascenders for numerals.
Old Style Roman	Type face with rounded serifs, numerals usually with ascenders and descenders.
Saccadic movements	In reading, the quick eye sweep from one fixation point to the next.
Serifs	Strokes, usually horizontal, at top and bottom of letters.
Tachistoscope	Special instrument to measure legibility by short-exposure method.
x-height	Visual size of letters, independent of actual body size.

Bibliography

1 Alderman, E. "The Effect of Size of Type on Speed of Reading and the Determination of Various Factors that May Influence the Results." **The Pittsburgh Schools,** 13 (November and December, 1938), 33-63.

2 Anderson, I. H., and Meredith, C. W. "The Reading of Projected Books with Special Reference to Rate and Visual Fatigue." **Journal of Educational Research,** 41 (February, 1948), 453-460.

3 Arps, R. B., Erdmann, R. L., Neal, A. S., and Schlaepfer, C. E. "Character Legibility Versus Resolution in Image Processing of Printed Matter." **IEEE Transaction, Man-Machine Systems,** (September 1969), 66-71.

4 Baird, J. W. "The Legibility of a Telephone Directory." **Journal of Applied Psychology,** 1 (March, 1917), 30-37.

5 Barnett, M. P.: **Computer Typesetting.** Cambridge, Mass.: The M.I.T. Press, 1965.

6 Bartz, B. S. "Type Variation and the Problem of Cartographic Legibility." **Journal of Typographic Research,** 3 (April, 1969), 127-144.

7 Bartz, B. S. "Search: An Approach to Cartographic Type Legibility Measurement." **Journal of Typographic Research,** 3 (October, 1969), 387-398.

8 Bartz, B. S. "Experimental Use of the Search Task in an Analysis of Type Legibility in Cartography." **Journal of Typographic Research,** 4 (Spring, 1970), 147-167.

9 Bass, R. "The Development of CBS News 36." **Journal of Typographic Research,** 4 (October, 1967), 357-372.

10 Bass, R. "The Development of Vidifont." **Visible Language,** 1 (Winter, 1971), 5-12.

11 Becker, D., Heinrich, J., Von Sichowsky, R., and Wendt, D. "Reader Preferences for Typeface and Leading." **Journal of Typographic Research,** 1 (Winter, 1970), 61-66.

12 Bell, H. M. "The Comparative Legibility of Typewriting, Manuscript, and Cursive Script: I. Easy Prose, Letters and Syllables." **Journal of Psychology,** 8 (October, 1939), 295-305.

13 Bell, H. M. "The Comparative Legibility of Typewriting, Manuscript, and Cursive Script: II. Difficult Prose and Eye-Movement Photography." **Journal of Psychology,** 8 (October, 1939), 311-320.

14 Bentley, M. "Leading and Legibility." **Psychological Monographs,** 30 (1921), 48-61.

15 Berger, C. "Stroke-Width, Form, and Horizontal Spacing of Numerals as Determinants of the Threshold of Recognition." **Journal of Applied Psychology,** 28 (June and August, 1944), 208-231, 336-346.

16 Berger, C. "Some Experiments on the Width of Symbols as Determinants of Legibility." **Acta Ophthalmologica,** 26 (1948), 517-550.

17 Betts, E. A. "Reading: Visual-Motor Skills." **Education,** 1968, 88 (4), 291-295.

18 Bonsiepe, G. "A Method of Quantifying Order in Typographic Design." **Journal of Typographic Research,** 3 (July, 1968), 203-220.

19 Breland, K., and Breland M. K. "Legibility of Newspaper Headlines Printed in Capitals and in Lower Case." **Journal of Applied Psychology,** 28 (April, 1944), 117-120.

20 Bridgman, C. S., and Wade, E. A. "Optimum Letter Size for a Given Display Area." **Journal of Applied Psychology,** 40 (December, 1956), 378-380.

21 Brown, W. S. "Speedreading Made Easy." **Journal of Typographic Research,** 1 (Winter, 1970), 73-75.

22 Burnhill, P. "Typographic Education: Headings in Text." **Journal of Typographic Research,** 4 (Autumn, 1970), 353-365.

23 Burt, Sir Cyril: **A Psychological Study of Typography.** Cambridge: University Press, 1959.

24 Burtt, H. E., and Basch, C. "Legibility of Bodoni, Baskerville Roman, and Cheltenham Type Faces." **Journal of Applied Psychology,** 7 (September, 1923), 237-245.

25 Burtt, H. E., Beck, H. C., and Campbell, E. "Legibility of Backbone Titles." **Journal of Applied Psychology,** 12 (April, 1928), 217-227.

26 Carver, R. P. "Effect of a 'Chunked' Typography on Reading Rate and Comprehension." **Journal of Applied Psychology,** 54 (June, 1970), 288-296.

27 Cheetham, D., Poulton, E. C., and Grimbly, B. "The Case for Research." **Design,** 195 (1965), 48-51.

28 Click, J. W., and Stempel, G. H. "Reader Response to Newspaper Front-Page Format." **Journal of Typographic Research,** 2 (April, 1968), 127-142.

29 Coleman, E. B., and Hahn, S. C. "Failure to Improve Legibility with a Vertical Typography." **Journal of Applied Psychology,** 50 (October, 1966), 434-436.

30 Coleman, E. B., and Kim, L. "Comparison of Several Styles of Typography in English." **Journal of Applied Psychology,** 45 (August, 1961), 262-267.

31 Crosland, H. H., and Johnson, G. "The Range of Apprehension as Affected by Inter-Letter Hair-Spacing and by the Characteristics of Individual Letters." **Journal of Applied Psychology,** 12 (February, 1928), 82-124.

32 Crouwel, W. "Type Design for the Computer Age," **Journal of Typographic Research,** 1 (Winter, 1970), 51-59.

33 Davenport, J. S., and Smith, S. A. "The Effect of Hyphenation, Justification, and Type Size on Newspaper Readability." **Journalism Quarterly,** 42 (Summer, 1965), 382-388.

34 Demilia, L. A. "Visual Fatigue and Reading." **Journal of Education,** 151 (1968), 4-24.

35 Didelot, M. "What Type Sizes and Measures Offer the Maximum Legibility?" **Inland Printer,** 88 (December, 1931), 35-37.

36 Dulsky, S. G. "Factors Influencing the Amount of Copy Read in Magazine Advertisements." **Journal of Applied Psychology,** 17 (April, 1933), 195-204.

37 Earhard, B. "Perception and Retention of Familiar and Unfamiliar Material." **Journal of Experimental Psychology,** 76 (1968), 584-595.

38   English, E. "A Study of the Legibility of Four Newspaper Headline Types." **Journalism Quarterly,** 21 (September, 1944), 217-229.

39   Erdmann, R. L., and Neal, A. S. "Character Legibility and Digital Facsimile Resolution." **Human Factors,** 10 (5, 1968), 465-474.

40   Erdmann, R. L., and Neal, A. S. "Word Legibility as a Function of Letter Legibility, with Word Size, Word Familiarity, and Resolution Parameters." **Journal of Applied Psychology,** 52 (October, 1968), 403-409.

41   Evers, C. H. "Adjustment to Unjustified Composition on the Rotterdamsch Nieuwsblad." **Journal of Typographic Research,** 1 (Winter, 1968), 59-74.

42   Fabrizio, R., Kaplan, L., and Teal, G. "Readability as a Function of the Straightness of Right-Hand Margins." **Journal of Typographic Research,** 1 (January, 1967), 90-95.

43   Fell, J. C., and Laughery, K. R. "Short-Term Memory: Mode of Presentation for Alphanumeric Information." **Human Factors,** 11 (1969), 401-406.

44   Fisher, P. "History of Type Readability Studies Discloses No 'Perfect' Type Face." **Inland Printer** (June, 1954), 66-67.

45   Foster, J. J. **Legibility Research Abstracts 1970.** London: Lund Humphries, 1970.

46   Foster, J. J. "A Study of the Legibility of One- and Two-Column Layouts for BPS Publications." **Bulletin of the British Psychological Society,** 23 (1970), 113-114.

47   Foster, J. J. "Directional Consistency in Form Identifcation." **Journal of Typographic Research,** 4 (Spring, 1970), 138-145.

48   Frase, L. T. "Tabular and Diagrammic Presentation of Verbal Materials." **Perceptual and Motor Skills,** 29 (1969), 320-322.

49   Frutiger, A. "Letterforms in Photo-Typography." **Journal of Typographic Research,** 4 (Autumn, 1970), 327-335.

50   Frutiger, A. "OCR-B: A Standardized Character for Optical Recognition." **Journal of Typographic Research,** 2 (April, 1967), 137-146.

51   Gilliland, A. R. "The Effect on Reading of Changes in the Size of Type." **Elementary School Journal,** 24 (October, 1923), 138-146.

52 Glanville, A. D., Kreezer, G. L., and Dallenbach, K. M. "The Effect of Type Size on Accuracy of Apprehension and Speed of Localizing Words." **American Journal of Psychology,** 59 (April, 1946), 220-235.

53 Gould, P. N., Raines, L. C., and Rucknick, C. A. "The Printing of Backbone Titles on Thin Books and Magazines." **Psychological Monographs,** 30 (1921), 62-67.

54 Gregory, M., and Poulton, E. C. "Even Versus Uneven Right-Margins and the Rate of Comprehension in Reading." **Ergonomics,** 13 (1970), 427-434.

55 Griffing, H., and Franz, S. I. "The Conditions of Fatigue in Reading." **Psychological Review,** 3 (September, 1896), 513-530.

56 Hackman, R. B., and Tinker, M. A. "Effect of Variations in Color of Print and Background Upon Eye Movements in Reading." **American Journal of Optometry and Archives of the American Academy of Optometry,** 34 (July, 1957), 354-359.

57 Hartley, J., and Burnhill, P. "Experiments with Unjustified Text." **Journal of Typographic Research,** 3 (Summer, 1971), 265-278.

58 Harrison, R., and Morris, C. D. J. "Communication Theory and Typographic Research." **Journal of Typographic Research,** 2 (April, 1967), 115-124.

59 Haskins, J. B. "Testing the Suitability of Type-Faces for Editorial Subject Matter." **Journalism Quarterly,** 35 (1958), 186-194.

60 Hinds, L. R., and Dodds, W. G. "Words in Color: Two Experimental Studies." **Journal of Typographic Research,** 1 (January, 1968), 43-52.

61 Hoffman, A. C. "Eye Movements During Prolonged Reading." **Journal of Experimental Psychology,** 36 (April, 1946), 95-118.

62 Holmes, G. "The Relative Legibility of Black Print and White Print." **Journal of Applied Psychology,** 15 (June, 1931), 248-251.

63 Horton, D. L., and Mecherikoff, M. "Letter Preferences: Ranking the Alphabet." **Journal of Applied Psychology,** 44 (August, 1960), 252-253.

64 Hovde, H. D. "The Relative Effect of Size of Type, Leading, and Context, Part II." **Journal of Applied Psychology,** 14 (February, 1930), 63-73.

65 Huey, E. B. "Preliminary Experiments in the Physiology and Psychology of Reading." **American Journal of Psychology,** 9 (July, 1898), 575-586.

66   Hurlburt, A. "A Modular Approach to Newspaper Design." **Graphis,** 156 (27), 418-421.

67   Hvistendahl, J. K. "Headline Readability Measured in Context." **Journalism Quarterly,** 38 (Spring, 1961), 226-228.

68   Jones, K. J. "A Research Report on Color Study Reading." **Journal of Typographic Research,** 1 (January, 1968), 53-56.

69   Kastl, J., and Child, I. L., "Emotional Meaning of Four Typographic Variables." **Journal of Applied Psychology,** 52 (1968), 440-446.

70   Klare, G. R., Nichols, W. H., and Shuford, E. H. "The Relationship of Typographic Arrangement to the Learning of Technical Training Material." **Journal of Applied Psychology,** 41 (February, 1957), 41-45.

71   Kolers, P. A. "Clues to a Letter's Recognition: Implications for the Design of Characters." **Journal of Typographic Research,** 2 (April, 1969), 145-168.

72   Lansdell, H. "Effects of Form on the Legibility of Numbers." **Canadian Journal of Psychology,** 8 (June, 1954), 77-79.

73   Lawson, A. "Scientific Attempts to Study Legibility." **Inland/American Printer,** 144 (1959), 364-367.

74   Lees, J., and Farman, M. "An Investigation of the Design and Performance of Traffic Control Devices." **Journal of Typographic Research,** 4 (Winter, 1970), 7-38.

75   Luckiesh, M., and Moss, F. K. "Boldness as a Factor in Type-Design and Typography." **Journal of Applied Psychology,** 24 (April, 1940), 170-183.

76   Luckiesh, M., and Moss, F. K. "Criteria of Readability." **Journal of Experimental Psychology,** 27 (September, 1940), 256-270.

77   Luckiesh, M., and Moss, F. K. "Effects of Leading on Legibility." **Journal of Applied Psychology,** 22 (April, 1938), 140-160.

78   Luckiesh, M., and Moss, F. K. "The Effect of Line Length on Readability." **Journal of Applied Psychology,** 25 (February, 1941), 67-75.

79   Luckiesh, M., and Moss, F. K. "The Extent of the Perceptual Span in Reading." **Journal of General Psychology,** 25 (October, 1941), 267-272.

80   Luckiesh, M., and Moss, F. K. "The Visibility of Print on Various Qualities of Paper." **Journal of Applied Psychology,** 25 (April, 1941), 152-158.

81 Luckiesh, M., and Moss, F. K. "The Visibility of Various Type Faces." **Journal of the Franklin Institute,** 223 (January, 1937), 77-82.

82 Mergenthaler Linotype Co.: **The Readability of Type.** New York: 1947.

83 Mergler, H. W., and Vargo, P. M. "One Approach to Computer Assisted Letter Design." **Journal of Typographic Research,** 2 (October, 1968), 299-322.

84 Montague, A. "Designing the Initial Teaching Alphabet in Five Type Faces."**Journal of Typographic Research,** 1 (Winter, 1970), 69-72.

85 Munson, J. H. "Computer Recognition of Hand-Printed Text." **Journal of Typographic Research,** 3 (January, 1969), 31-61.

86 Nashinsky, I. D. "The Influence of Certain Typographical Arrangements Upon Span of Visual Comprehension." **Journal of Applied Psychology,** 40 (February, 1956), 37-39.

87 Neman, T. E. "The Relative Legibility of three Cold Type Faces, three Line Lengths, three Paper Stocks, and the Interaction of these three Variables." **Unpublished Ph.D. dissertation,** Indiana University, 1968.

88 North, A. J., and Jenkins, L. B. "Reading Speed and Comprehension as a Function of Typography." **Journal of Applied Psychology,** 35 (August, 1951), 225-228.

89 Ovink, G. W.: **Legibility, Atmosphere-Value and Forms of Printing Types.** Leiden: A. W. Sitjthoff's Uitgeversmaatschappij N. V., 1938.

90 Paterson, D. G., and Tinker, M. A. "Capitals Versus Lower Case in Headlines." **Editor and Publisher,** 75 (1941), 51.

91 Paterson, D. G., and Tinker, M. A. "Eye Movements in Reading Optimal and Non-Optimal Typography." **Journal of Experimental Psychology,** 34 (February, 1944), 80-83.

92 Paterson, D. G., and Tinker, M. A. "Eye Movements in Reading Type Sizes in Optimal Line Widths." **Journal of Educational Psychology,** 34 (December, 1943), 547-551.

93 Paterson, D. G., and Tinker, M. A.: **How To Make Type Readable.** New York: Harper & Brothers, Publishers, 1940.

94 Paterson, D. G., and Tinker, M. A. "Influence of Leading Upon the Readability of Newspaper Type." **Journal of Applied Psychology,** 31 (April, 1947), 160-163.

71

95 Paterson, D. G., and Tinker, M. A. "Influence of Line Width on Eye Movements." **Journal of Experimental Psychology,** 27 (November, 1940), 572-577.

96 Paterson, D. G., and Tinker, M. A. "Influence of Line Width on Eye Movements for Six Point Type." **Journal of Educational Psychology,** 33 (October, 1942), 552-555.

97 Paterson, D. G., and Tinker, M. A. "Influence of Size of Type on Eye Movements." **Journal of Applied Psychology,** 26 (April, 1942), 227-230.

98 Paterson, D. G., and Tinker, M. A. "Readability of Newspaper Headlines Printed in Capitals and Lower Case." **Journal of Applied Psychology,** 30 (April, 1946), 161-168.

99 Paterson, D. G., and Tinker, M. A. "Studies of Typographical Factors Influencing Speed of Reading: II. Size of Type." **Journal of Applied Psychology,** 13 (April, 1929), 120-130.

100 Paterson, D. G., and Tinker, M. A. "Studies of Typographical Factors Influencing Speed of Reading: IV. Effect of Practice on Equivalence of Test Forms." **Journal of Applied Psychology,** 14 (June, 1930), 211-217.

101 Paterson, D. G., and Tinker, M. A. "Studies of Typographical Factors Influencing Speed of Reading: VI. Black Type Versus White Type." **Journal of Applied Psychology,** 15 (June, 1931), 241-247.

102 Paterson, D. G., and Tinker, M. A. "Studies of Typographical Factors Influencing Speed of Reading: VIII. Space Between Lines or Leading." **Journal of Applied Psychology,** 16 (August, 1932), 388-397.

103 Paterson, D. G., and Tinker, M. A. "Studies of Typographical Factors Influencing Speed of Reading: X. Style of Type Face." **Journal of Applied Psychology,** 16 (December, 1932), 605-613.

104 Paterson, D. G., and Tinker, M. A. "The Effect of Typography Upon the Perceptual Span in Reading." **American Journal of Psychology,** 60 (July, 1947), 388-396.

105 Paterson, D. G., and Tinker, M. A. "The Part-Whole Proportion Illusion in Printing." **Journal of Applied Psychology,** 22 (August, 1938), 421-425.

106 Paterson, D. G., and Tinker, M. A. "The Relative Legibility of Newsprint and Book Print." **Journal of Applied Psychology,** 30 (October, 1946), 454-459.

107 Payne, D. E. "Readability of Typewritten Material: Proportional Versus Standard Spacing." **Journal of Typographic Research,** 2 (April, 1967), 125-136.

108 Perry, D. K. "Speed and Accuracy of Reading Arabic and Roman Numerals." **Journal of Applied Psychology,** 36 (October, 1952), 346-347.

109 Poffenberger, A. T., and Franken, R. B. "Appropriateness of Type Faces." **Journal of Applied Psychology,** 7 (December, 1923), 312-329.

110 Poulton, E. C. "Letter Differentiation and Rate of Comprehension of Reading." **Journal of Applied Psychology,** 49 (1955), 358-362.

111 Pratt, C. C. "A Note on the Legibility of Items in a Bibliography." **Journal of Applied Psychology,** 8 (April, 1924), 362-364.

112 Preston, K., Schwankl, H. P., and Tinker, M. A. "The Effect of Variations in Color of Print and Background on Legibility." **Journal of General Psychology, 6** (April, 1932), 459-461.

113 Rehe, R. F. "Psychological Studies and Their Impact on Modern Typography." **Inland Printer/American Lithographer,** part I, March 1970, 53; part II, April, 1970, 66.

114 Rice, S. "A Standard Code for Special Typographic Character Identification." **Journal of Typographic Research,** 3 (April, 1969), 183-192.

115 Robinson, D. O., Abbamonte, M., and Evans, S. H. "Why Serifs Are Important: the Perception of Small Print." **Visible Language,** 4 (Autumn, 1971), 353-359.

116 Roethlein, B. E. "The Relative Legibility of Different Faces of Printing Type." **American Journal of Psychology,** 23 (January, 1912), 1-36.

117 Ruder, E.: **Typography.** Teufen (Switzerland): Arthur Niggli, 1967.

118 Sanford, E. C. "The Relative Legibility of the Small Letters." **American Journal of Psychology,** 1 (May, 1968), 402-435.

119 Schiller, W. "Wirkungsmoeglichkeiten der Typografie." **Druckformherstellung,** 22 (June, 1971), 81-85.

120 Schulz-Anker, E.: **Formanalyse und Dokumentation einer seriflosen Linearschrift auf neuer Basis: Syntax-Antiqua.** Frankfurt/Main: D. Stempel AG., 1969.

121 Scorsone, J. S. "Ligature Design for Contemporary Technology." **Journal of Typographic Research,** 1 (Winter, 1970), 39-50.

122 Seybold, J. W. "Esthetic Values in Computerized Photo-Composition." **Journal of Typographic Research,** 2 (October, 1968), 341-350.

123 Shurtleff, D. "Relative Legibility of Leroy and Lincoln/MITRE Fonts on Television." **Journal of Typographic Research,** 1 (January, 1969), 79-89.

124 Skordahl, D. M. "Effect of Sloping Text Upon the Speed of Reading and Upon Visibility." **Unpublished paper,** University of Minnesota, 1958.

125 Smith, F., Lott, D., and Cronnel, B. "The Effect of Size and Case Alternation on Word Identification." **American Journal of Psychology,** 82 (1969), 248-253.

126 Soar, R. S. "Readability of Typography in Psychological Journals." **Journal of Applied Psychology,** 35 (February, 1951), 64-67.

127 Spencer, H.: **the visible word.** London: Lund Humphries, 1968.

128 Stanton, F. N., and Burtt, H. E. "The Influence of Surface and Tint of Paper on Speed of Reading." **Journal of Applied Psychology,** 19 (December, 1935), 683-693.

129 Strong, E. K. "Values of White Space in Advertising." **Journal of Applied Psychology,** 10 (March, 1926), 107-116.

130 Sumner, F. K. "Influence of Color on Legibility of Copy." **Journal of Applied Psychology,** 16 (April, 1932), 201-204.

131 Taylor, C. D. "The Relative Legibility of Black and White Print." **Journal of Educational Psychology,** 25 (November, 1934), 561-578.

132 Tannenbaum, P. H., Jacobson, H. K., and Norris, E. L. "An Experimental Investigation of Typeface Connotations." **Journalism Quarterly,** 41 (Winter, 1964), 65-73.

133 Teal, G. E., Kaplan, I. T., Payne, D. E., and Hollstein, F. "Readability as a Function of the Straightness of Right-Hand Margins." Abstract in **U.S. Government Research and Development Reports** (Report No. AD-425-150).

134 Telingater, S. B. "The Standardization of Alphabetic Graphemes." **Journal of Typographic Research,** 2 (July, 1968), 233-240.

135 Tinker, M. A.: **Bases for Effective Reading.** Minneapolis: University of Minnesota Press, 1965.

136 Tinker, M. A. "Criteria for Determining the Readability of Type Faces." **Journal of Educational Psychology,** 36 (October, 1946), 453-460.

137   Tinker, M. A. "Cumulative Effect of Marginal Conditions Upon Rate of Perception in Reading." **Journal of Applied Psychology,** 32 (October, 1948), 537-540.

138   Tinker, M. A. "Effect of Angular Alignment Upon Readability of Print." **Journal of Educational Psychology,** 47 (October, 1956), 358-363.

139   Tinker, M. A. "Effect of Curved Text Upon Readability of Print." **Journal of Applied Psychology,** 41 (April, 1957), 218-221.

140   Tinker, M. A. "Legibility of Mathematical Tables." **Journal of Applied Psychology,** 44 (April, 1960), 83-87.

141   Tinker, M. A.: **Legibility of Print.** Ames, Iowa: Iowa State University Press, 1969.

142   Tinker, M. A. "Length of Work Periods in Visual Research." **Journal of Applied Psychology,** 42 (October, 1958), 343-345.

143   Tinker, M. A. "Numerals Versus Words for Efficiency in Reading." **Journal of Applied Psychology,** 12 (April, 1928), 190-199.

144   Tinker, M. A. "Perceptual and Oculomotor Efficiency in Reading Materials in Vertical and Horizontal Arrangements." **American Journal of Psychology,** 68 (September, 1955), 444-449.

145   Tinker, M. A. "Prolonged Reading Tasks in Visual Research." **Journal of Applied Psychology,** 39 (December, 1955), 444-446.

146   Tinker, M. A. "Readability of Mathematical Tables." **Journal of Applied Psychology,** 38 (December, 1954), 436-442.

147   Tinker, M. A. "Suitable Typography for Beginners in Reading." **Education,** 88 (1968), 317-320.

148   Tinker, M. A. "The Influence of Form of Type on the Perception of Words." **Journal of Applied Psychology,** 16 (April, 1932), 167-174.

149   Tinker, M. A. "The Relative Legibility of the Letters, the Digits, and of Certain Mathematical Signs." **Journal of General Psychology,** 1 (July-October, 1928), 472-496.

150   Tinker, M. A. "The Relative Legibility of Modern and Old Style Numerals." **Journal of Experimental Psychology,** 13 (October, 1930), 453-461.

151   Tinker, M. A. "Time Relations for Eye Movement Measures in Reading." **Journal of Educational Psychology,** 38 (January, 1947), 1-10.

152   Tinker, M. A., and Paterson, D. G. "Differences Among Newspaper Body Types in Readability." **Journalism Quarterly,** 20 (June, 1943), 152-155.

153   Tinker, M. A., and Paterson, D. G. "Effect of Line Width and Leading on Readability of Newspaper Type." **Journalism Quarterly,** 23 (September, 1946), 307-309.

154   Tinker, M. A., and Paterson, D. G. "Influence of Simultaneous Variation in Size of Type, Width of Line, and Leading for Newspaper Type." **Journal of Applied Psychology,** 47 (1963), 380-382.

155   Tinker, M. A., and Paterson, D. G. "Influence of Type Forms on Eye Movements." **Journal of Experimental Psychology,** 25 (November, 1939), 528-531.

156   Tinker, M. A., and Paterson, D. G. "Influence of Type Form on Speed of Reading." **Journal of Applied Psychology,** 12 (August, 1928), 359-368.

157   Tinker, M. A., and Paterson, D. G. "Readability of Mixed Type Forms." **Journal of Applied Psychology,** 30 (December, 1946), 631-637.

158   Tinker, M. A., and Paterson, D. G. "Reader Preferences and Typography." **Journal of Applied Psychology,** 26 (February, 1942), 38-40.

159   Tinker, M. A., and Paterson, D. G. "Speed of Reading Nine Point Type in Relation to Line Width and Leading." **Journal of Applied Psychology,** 33 (February, 1949), 81-82.

160   Tinker, M. A., and Paterson, D. G. "Studies of Typographical Factors Influencing Speed of Reading: III. Length of Line." **Journal of Applied Psychology,** 13 (June, 1929), 205-219.

161   Tinker, M. A., and Paterson, D. G. "Studies of Typographical Factors Influencing Speed of Reading: V. Simultaneous Variation of Type Size and Line Length." **Journal of Applied Psychology,** 15 (February, 1931), 72-78.

162   Tinker, M. A., and Paterson, D. G. "Studies of Typographical Factors Influencing Speed of Reading: VII. Variations in Color of Print and Background." **Journal of Applied Psychology,** 15 (October, 1931), 471-479.

163   Tinker, M. A., and Paterson, D. G. "Studies of Typographical Factors Influencing Speed of Reading: IX. Reduction in Size of Newspaper Print." **Journal of Applied Psychology,** 16 (October, 1932), 525-531.

164   Tinker, M. A., and Paterson, D. G. "Studies of Typographical Factors Influencing Speed of Reading: XI. Role of Set in Typographical Studies." **Journal of Applied Psychology,** 19 (December, 1935), 647-651.

165   Tinker, M. A., and Paterson, D. G. "Studies of Typographical Factors Influencing Speed of Reading: XIII. Methodological Considerations." **Journal of Applied Psychology,** 20 (February, 1936), 132-145.

166   Tinker, M. A., and Paterson, D. G. "Wartime Changes in Newspaper Body Type." **Journalism Quarterly,** 21 (March, 1944), 7-11.

167   Tomaszewski, R. "Die Forschungsarbeiten zur Lesbarkeit gedruckter Texte muessen beschleunigt werden." **Druckformenherstellung,** 22 (June, 1971), 93-96 (transl. from the Polish).

168   Truex, J. W. "A Study of Reading Times and Reader Preferences When Line Length and Alphabet Length Are Simultaneously and Directly Varied." **Unpublished M.S. Thesis,** South Dakota State University, 1966.

169   Turnbull, A. T., and Carter, D. E. "Readership of Advertisements With All-Display Typography." **Journal of Typographic Research,** 2 (April, 1968), 157-169.

170   Troxel, D. "Automated Reading of the Printed Page." **Visible Language,** 2 (Spring, 1971), 125-144.

171   Uhlaner, J. E. "The Thickness of Stroke on the Legibility of Letters." **Proceedings of the Iowa Academy of Science,** 48 (1941), 319-324.

172   Uschakowa, M. N. "Die Messbarkeit und Moeglichkeit der Kontrolle der Lesegeschwindigkeit." **Druckformherstellung,** 22 (June, 1971), 87-89 (transl. from the Russian).

173   Vartabedian, A. G. "A Proposed Fontstyle for the Graphic Presentation of the Oh and Zero." **Journal of Typographic Research,** 3 (July, 1969), 249-258.

174   Vernon, M. D.: **III. Studies in the Psychology of Reading: A. The Errors Made in Reading.** London: H. M. Stationery Office, (1929), 5-36.

175   Webster, H. A., and Tinker, M. A. "The Influence of Paper Surface on the Perceptibility of Print." **Journal of Applied Psychology,** 19 (April, 1935), 145-147.

176   Webster, H. A., and Tinker, M. A. "The Influence of Type Face on the Legibility of Print." **Journal of Applied Psychology,** 19 (February, 1935), 43-52.

177   Wendt, D. "Lesen und Lesbarkeit in Abhaengigkeit von der Textanordnung." **Druckformenherstellung,** 22 (June, 1971), 90-92.

178   Wendt, D. "O or 0?" **Journal of Typographic Research,** 3 (July, 1969), 241-248.

179   Wendt, D. "Probleme und Ergebnisse psychologischer Lesbarkeitsforschung." **Druck-Print,** 107 (1970), 16-19.

180   Wendt, D. "Semantic Differentials of Typefaces as a Method of Congeniality Research." **Journal of Typographic Research,** 1 (January, 1968), 3-25.

181   Wiggins, R. H. "Effects of Three Typographical Variables on Speed of Reading." **Journal of Typographic Research,** 1 (January, 1967), 5-18.

182   Wrolstad, M. E. "Adult Preferences in Typography: Exploring the Function of Design." **Journalism Quarterly,** 37 (Winter, 1960), 211-223.

183   Zachrisson, B.: **Studies in the Legibility of Printed Text.** Stockholm: Almqvist & Wiksell, 1965.

184   Zapf, H. "Changes in Letterforms Due to Technical Developments." **Journal of Typographic Research,** 4 (October, 1968), 351-368.

Typesetting: Rogers Typesetting Company, Inc., Indianapolis
Paper: C. P. Lesh Paper Company, Indianapolis